AI Poetry

Kimberly Flomerfelt-Puc

BookLeaf
Publishing

India | USA | UK

Presentation by *BookLeaf Publishing*

Web: www.bookleafpub.com

E-mail: info@bookleafpub.com

ISBN: 9789360947323

First edition 2024

For my family

ACKNOWLEDGEMENT

A most grateful thank you to my wonderful husband for his unwavering support.

Wild

Solitude reared us,

in nature's embrace.

Harsh yet delicate,

our adventures unbound.

Fear cowered in shadows,

as our backyard bloomed.

Love and nourishment scarce,

we relied on each other.

Clever schemes to endure,

bonding us through struggle.

But division crept in,

separating and sorrowing.

Yet, we toughened our skin,

learning to thrive.

Through tribulations, we rose anew,

united as a resilient crew.

Forgiveness, a crucial key,

to manifest the best destiny.

Proudly, we've weathered the years,

our bond unwavering, our love dear.

Late Bloomer

Amidst the chaos, a child thrives,

Clings to family and finds her drive.

Through adversity and pain, she grows,

A late bloomer, but her spirit glows.

Challenges come, but she's undeterred,

With familiarity and strength, she's spurred.

Her journey continues with each new day,

And love, true and pure, comes her way.

She blossoms into an optimistic force,

Inspiring others with her unbreakable course.

Leaving a mark on this world, so bright,

Caring for the little things with all her might.

As time goes on, she dreams of leaving behind,

A legacy of love and joy, in her kind.

But until then, she'll keep living her best,

Making her impact, before she rests.

Birth

Imagining the arrival of her first child,

Her heart brims with hope and love.

Tiny fingers and toes dance in her dreams,

As she envisions pure joy and unconditional love.

The day arrives, she celebrates her birth,

Her precious one emerges as the most beautiful sight.

And as the sun sets on this blessed day,

She cradles her son in loving arms.

Gazing upon his beauty, so small and new,

Her heart overflows with delight.

His smile, his laughter, fill her with joy,

As she dreams of all that he will be.

Not long after, baby number two joins the fold,

And with equal fervor, she welcomes another son.

Her firstborn is now a big brother, inseparable they grow,

Together they journey through life's highs and lows.

Now grown and ready to start their own families,

She watches with pride and admiration aplenty.

For the love she planted has blossomed into more,

A legacy of love for generations to come.

Libby

On a frigid morning, we embarked on a ride,

My father at the helm, his rig in full stride.

Beside my siblings, I perched with pride,

As the grandeur of nature took center stage.

A sudden blur, a dog and boy in sight,

My dad swerved to avoid their tragic plight.

But on black ice, our truck took flight,

And in the ditch, we met an untimely date.

The engine roared as we landed in a snowy
ditch,

I unfolded myself, now at my father's feet.

Blessed with only some scrapes to tell the tale,

We knew fate had spared us.

Strangers arrived, lending their aid,

They expected the outcome to be grim.

But my protector stayed serene, caring, and
strong,

For with him at our side, we were not afraid.

Figaro Todd, The Noodle Cat

Figaro Todd, the noodle cat,

Best little kitty in the whole world devine.

The feline queen of all things fine.

With grace and poise, she roamed her lair,

And watched the world with her greenish stare.

She ruled the house with gentle might,

A mother to all in her sight.

Peaches and Cleo, her dear kin,

Protected by Figaro's loving skin.

Her spirit was wild, untamed, and free,

Exploring nature's endless sea.

But never did she stray too far,

For her home was where her heart would mar.

Nine lives she lived, each one well spent,

Till the time came for her final ascent.

But her legacy will forever remain,

In our hearts, her name shall reign.

So here's to Figaro Todd, the noodle cat fair,

Forever our beloved feline heir.

Ode to Dartmouth

I'm in love,

With Sacajawea.

If she needed me to

I'd move to Korea

for Sacajawea.

Thick black hair.

waving in the air so fair,

I would be her Fred Astaire,

her mountain or her polar bear.

When she walks slowly down

the river,

I would do anything to be with her.

The way that she walks, and stumbles,

it's as if she could fly.

"I miss you" I mumble.

She is with the trees,

I am on my knees,

Begging her to please

Return from her journey,

To me.

My beloved Sacajawea.

Travelers

In a time long ago, two brothers dwelled,

Amidst the lush mossy mountains, they excelled.

With clever minds, that spoke all tongues,

They built machines to travel through distant
runs.

And with this power, they sought to aid,

Those in need who were afraid.

One day, a note of code was found,

And a plea from a dinosaur family resound.

Without hesitation, they packed their machine,

To journey back to the Jurassic scene.

Fields of extinct beings greeted their eyes,

A breathtaking sight beneath the skies.

A Pterodactyl offered transport to the valley below,

Where they learned how to help and where to go.

With calculations and wit, they found the lost egg,

Bringing joy and relief to the family's nest.

But moving it proved to be a new trial,

Yet nothing could stop these brothers' guile.

Reunited, they all bid farewell,

As the brothers returned home, with more tales to tell.

Their hearts full of hope for their next quest,

To help those in need, and do their best.

Star Route 10

In the great northern wild,

Where snowcapped mountains scrape the sky,

A winding path leads

To a patch of currants and blueberries.

We chased the swift ptarmigan,

And braved the river's flow.

A reminder to whistle,

Our only guard against grizzlies, we know.

Nature and kindness provide all we need,

On this boundless adventure.

Soft mossy grounds,

Tickle our bare feet.

Basking in the summer sun

That never fades.

We make camp under starry skies,

And shared stories and food by the fire.

A simple life, but one of pure bliss,

As nature cares for us.

And when we choose

To brave treacherous roads,

Our bond grows stronger,

United as one gritty force.

Through hardship,

We learn faith,

And gain pride in our legacy.

Life

A young soul sent far from home,

Amidst walls of stone, all alone,

Dreams of returning were bittersweet,

For sisters surrounded, yet felt incomplete.

With empty halls and longing to flee,

Closed doors echoed lost possibility.

But fate's twist would not be ignored,

And a clever escape was soon scored.

By some miracle, safety was found.

Only to discover she had become a bound.

Alone in the chaos, fighting within,

A peace she sought to make.

But the cycle began again,

Lost and aimless, her drive slipped away,

Feeling undeserving, a weight to stay,

But a guardian force appeared in disguise,

Teaching caring for others, can fill the void inside.

Amidst trials and tears, rewards were found,

And through it all, inspiration was profound.

Love

Love's first touch, a breathless delight,

A feeling unknown, now shining so bright.

In an embrace, two souls become one,

No force can undo what love has begun.

A fleeting glance ignites the fire,

Never to tame the awakening desire,

Finding someone who loves me come what may,

Is the perfect part of every day.

In your arms, all worries disappear.

Each moment spent together, forever dear.

Love's precious gift, so pure and rare

With you by my side, nothing to compare.

And every day, I am grateful anew.

To be in love, with no one but you.

Homeward

The journey homeward, wrought with despair,

An unforgiving road, with no room to spare.

On day one, a crash befalls our fate,

Blocking the way for oncoming freight.

Engine trouble strikes, not once, but twice,

Costly and lengthy, it tests our might.

And then came illness to plague our crew,

Uncertainty looms, will we see this through?

Stranded in a land far from our own,

Where luck is our only faithful companion
known.

Trials upon trials, test our resolve,

Should we turn back? Our doubts evolve.

But just when all seemed bleak and dim,

A warm chinook wind and northern lights within.

Separated mid-west, with no aid in sight,

Lost communication in our time of plight.

Yet we rally together, strangers lending a hand,

Guided by Grandma's clever and tireless plan.

She stayed up all night making calls without rest,

Describing her lost son to anyone who'd listen best.

Our joy knows no bounds as we are reunited at last,

Roaring like thunder into a safe home at last.

Lessons learned in kindness and faith,

In unity and grit, never giving in to wraith.

Fort

Constructed from a fallen fence,

with a perfect view of the sunset,

And a sturdy bench.

A place to play guitar,

and ponder what is next,

A place to dream,

and put life into context.

Cleverly built, blended into the scene,

A place to have a snack,

Or escape to the serene.

The effort to build,

calmed the soul,

And distracted,

From life's bitter toll.

The order to deconstruct,

was met with dismay,

But the sturdy old fort,

Had served in its day.

Fort V2

Crafted from a crumbled fence,

A front-row seat to the sunset's glow,

Our haven, upon a sturdy bench.

Strumming guitars and contemplating what's in tow.

A space for dreaming and putting life in perspective,

Merged harmoniously with nature's grace,

A sanctuary for snacks or peaceful introspective,

As he built, his soul found solace in this place.

But alas, the time came to tear it down,

A twinge of sadness upon bidding adieu,

For his fort was more than just wood on the ground,

It held memories dear, as all good things do.

Dr. Laidlaw

Four girls played on the see-saw, hands intertwined,

But one let go and another fell behind.

Her arm twisted, a strange sight to see,

Her siblings consoled her until help could be.

Found in a distant town, a two-hour ride

A cowboy doctor came to her side.

With skilled hands, he mended her broken bone,

But when she awoke, she felt alone.

No longer a baby, but still needing care,

Her father's gentle touch wiped away her despair.

Together they traveled back to their home,

With memories of the kind cowboy who had shone.

Mol

A mother who grew up too fast,

Caring for siblings, grieving her past.

Her life was filled with loss and pain,

But she found her purpose as a nurse to sustain.

Betrothed to one, but fate intervened,

She met my father and their love intervened.

Together they built a family so large,

With six babies in eight years to charge.

But fate struck again, and she had to flee,

Distraught and burdened, she succumbed to
agony.

For years she remained broken and lost,

Until a chance to make things right at last.

But the demons within her could not be tamed,

And once again her life became maimed.

Her children returned, one by one,

But her time on earth was already done.

In ten short years, she made amends,

Forgiving and forgetting, cherishing the good trends.

For one thing, was certain, her love knew no bounds,

Though her start may have been rough,

It's the whole, that astounds.

His Skill

A man of noble heart and steady hands,

He studied his craft, fulfilling his plans.

For his family's sake, he worked with care,

Providing a comfortable life that he could share.

Generosity ran deep in his veins,

Treating those in need without any gains.

A pony for a crown? No payment required,

His kindness and selflessness never expired.

His skill brought comfort, no turning back,

He did his best to keep everything on track.

Chipped tooth or porcupine quills,

He mended them all, without any frills.

Not just a healer of physical wounds,

But an advisor, spreading wisdom around.

Retirement came but he stayed on,

For turning people away was something he couldn't condone.

With every patient, his goal remained clear,

To treat is to care,

His hands we hold dear.

My Father's Greenhouse

Tucked in a meadow, where tall grasses sway,

Stands a handmade greenhouse, enduring every
fray.

Through storms and repairs, it remains steadfast,

A sanctuary for plants, a world unsurpassed.

Inside, old propane tanks and a cast iron burner,

Remnants of stories shared, of resilience that
never falters.

For within these walls, lessons are sown,

Of triumph over hardship, and growth unknown.

Each plant is lovingly labeled, with a story to
tell,

My father tends to them with patience as his
spell.

From heirloom tomatoes to sunflowers tall,

Every seed's journey he knows, from start to fall.

With a skilled hand and heart full of grace,

He nurtures his garden, a most humble place.

For he grows not just crops, but something
more,

An offering of nourishment that our souls adore.

Bonus

Two precious gifts bestowed upon me,

filling my days with pure delight.

My heart, once content,

now overflows with love's endless might.

Then my path led me to another,

and three more blessings came my way.

Each one a shining star in their own right,

making me proud each passing day.

As I dream about the years ahead,

of the families they'll invent,

My love for them knows no bounds,

it's depth only grows with intent.

For Elise

At five years old, my first memory takes shape,

She stands tall, in control of our fate.

It would have been easier to simply not care,

But she gave her all, to show us she's there.

Teaching me strength and the joy in simple
things.

Making cookies by the hundreds, holiday joy
she brings.

Unforgettable meals, cooked with love and
grace,

Instilling self-sufficiency, a trait I now embrace.

Without even knowing, she drew for me to see,

A stepmom is a role so difficult to be.

You are often seen as a rival, unwelcome from
the start,

But then learn, it's impossible to escape the love
that grows in your heart.

www.ingramcontent.com/pod-product-compliance
Lightning Source LLC
LaVergne TN
LVHW010926200726

843509LV00013B/2091